THE S⟨

of HOPE

THE SONG
of HOPE

PSALMS AND MEDITATIONS FOR TODAY

Judith PINHEY

Text copyright © Judith Pinhey 2002
Illustations copyright © Ray Burrows 2002
The author asserts the moral right
to be identified as the author of this work

Published by
The Bible Reading Fellowship
First Floor, Elsfield Hall
15–17 Elsfield Way, Oxford OX2 8FG
ISBN 1 84101 261 0

First published 2002
10 9 8 7 6 5 4 3 2 1 0

A catalogue record for this book is available from the British Library

Printed and bound in Great Britain by
Bookmarque, Croydon

CONTENTS

FOREWORD

A song for every season, both natural and spiritual, and a reason for hope in every human experience—this is the promise that is fulfilled in the pages of this moving collection of one woman's 'psalms' offered first to her own faith community and now, happily, to a much wider readership.

Psalms make space for every shade of emotion and response, and Judith's psalms also lead us through the changing seasons—rejoicing in the thaws of spring and summer's flamboyant energy, the glory and the nakedness of autumn and the patient waiting of winter. Joy and regret, exuberance and loneliness—all are woven into a tapestry of praise that has the power to earth our liturgical prayer in the soil of our common experience.

Jesus the beachcomber gathers the detritus of ourselves and refashions us 'with an artist's eye'. God the sculptor brings our true selves forth from the chaos of our ordinary days. Peace falls upon us at Christmas 'like a bombshell' as God enters the cocoon of human life, tightly bound in swaddling clothes, to be at one with us in the eternal process of transformation. May Judith's gift of articulating these seasons of living and believing empower all her readers to discover, and rejoice in, their own soul seasons.

Margaret Silf

INTRODUCTION

I have chosen the meditations in this book from a much larger number that I have written during the last ten years. I have been making one available each week at my parish church, St James', Cambridge, and I usually base these writings on one or more of the Sunday readings or on the psalm. Apart from this discipline, which provides me with a variety of themes, I write about any aspect of the Christian faith that attracts my attention.

I write the meditations as poems because I enjoy this form. I like the patterns of rhymes and rhythms, the concision, the opportunity to play with words and images, the heightened tension and the interwoven layers of meaning.

I am an Anglican, but I also owe a great deal to several other Christian traditions. God's grace—his unlimited and unfailing love shown in Jesus Christ crucified and risen—is at the heart of my faith. I try to see everything in creation as bearing the mark of the cross, pointing to God and interpreting to us his nature and what he has done. Sometimes I see creation momentarily transfigured by his presence. I use aspects of creation as images of God's love and his nearness to us. All images are inadequate, but God has made himself accessible to us in Jesus, and I regard images used in this way as following from his willingness to become human. We can see eternity through what is temporal and recognize transcendence through what is material.

The song of hope is a song we can sing even when we look at the pain and destruction which are all too real in the natural world and in our lives. We are caught, now, between frustration and hope, but the cross of frustration is God's glory and it is the hope of glory for us.

Hope is a lovely gift, raising our hearts to God in thanksgiving, but it must be realistic hope, not false optimism. Christian hope is not hoping against hope. It is a firm hope because it depends, not on our human nature or circumstances, nor on the avoidance of the harshness of reality, but on God's love which is faithful love—love that never gives up, love that holds us whatever happens, love that knows what we are like and still goes on loving us to the uttermost, whether we know it or not. I offer these meditations in the hope that they may communicate this good news and the joy it brings.

I have arranged the meditations in four sections, named for the seasons of the year. Within these sections I have placed them where they fit according to the calendar year and the Church's year.

'Lord' always refers to Jesus in the meditations. Many of them are written as prayers to him.

I am grateful to all who have helped me in my faith and in my writing over the years. I should especially like to thank our vicar David Deboys for his inspiration and encouragement.

SPRING

THE WORD

Wait while
I think of
the word—
it's on
the tip
of my tongue...

It's a ladder
with only
one rung;
a perfectly
tuned
instrument,
tightly
strung;
the belfry
where God's
love
was hung;
a cry
of anguish
heavenward
flung;
a fire
that burns
dung;
a song
that every
human heart
has sung.

LENT

By Lent is meant
the lengthening
of the days
and the strengthening
in us of God's ways.

When I was young
and my song was unsung,
the days used to last
a sunlit age before they passed
and the time for play was spent.

Now the days go by
before I can breathe a sigh.
I am being changed
like a caterpillar that is rearranged
by hidden urges
within a chrysalis, and emerges
as a butterfly,
a brilliant newcomer
whose life does not last one summer.

So I will not catch anything that flies,
or snatch at its small frame,
or brush away the dust that clings
to its delicate wings.
For Jesus came
with mercy for everything that dies,
and he will raise
us and all creation to sing his praise.
Then our ways will be God's ways.

THE COLOUR OF REPENTANCE

Lord, in watching and waiting
I lay myself open to your call.
In receiving you I receive all.

Yet I am like a small
vase that remains empty
under the strong force
of the water that gushes
from a tap without remorse.

Be gentle with me.
If you come in mercy,
drop by drop, like the rain,
I shall receive what I can contain.
Even a small vase can hold violets
and keep them freshly in bloom,
so that the colour of repentance
may grace a room.

Violets are not flamboyant;
they grow close to the ground,
quietly concealed
by leaves at the foot of the birch.
They are not easily found.
Only to one who will search
carefully, who kneels to gaze,
is the heart of the flower revealed
against a purple frame,
its white rays
shaped like the wings of a bird,
its golden spur like a flame.

LIVING STONES

A stone is unprepossessing and obscure.
Its existence witnesses to the passing
of the ages, to a hidden crystalline
structure, to the movement of the earth,
to a violent new birth
from a cataclysmic event. It lies
in the hand, hard enough to endure.

Brown stones praise Christ,
who, tempted in the wilderness,
argued that God's word sufficed.
He refused to turn stones into bread,
defending their integrity,
content to become bread himself instead.

White stones praise Christ,
who, on behalf of all sinners
whom condemnation has enticed,
searched our hearts with this proposal:
'Let anyone who is without sin throw
the first stone.' With the same
grace he gives to each a white stone
on which is written a new name
that no one else can know.

Living stones of every colour,
dry, dull and mundane,
teach us something about renewal,
showing us how each is transformed
into a bright, shining jewel
by every shower of rain.

THE NAKED TRUTH

What did you go out into the wilderness to see?
A breeze playing in the branches of a thorn tree?
But what did you go out to see?
The posturing of the cognoscenti?
So what did you go out to see? A king
whose glory is to possess everything?

He has no jewels set with defiant skill,
vainglory to be put on and taken off at will,
knowledge calculated to bring the world to a standstill
with its conspicuous overkill.
His cross of gold is not an ornament,
for in him God's riches are well spent.

We twist thorns into a crown and flout
God's love. 'Crucify him!' is our repeated shout.
Naked he came into the world and naked he went out,
trusting God in the humiliation of doubt.
And still we go out into the wilderness to find
the naked truth of God and humankind.

MOTHERING GOD

I love you, mothering
God, never smothering
me, but setting me free
to become my true self, to grow, to be.

I live in the tension
between your non-intervention,
awe-inspiring in its mystery,
and your participation in our human history.

I leave my future to your will.
My past, redeemed, is with me still,
and the present resounds with one
reality: the glory of what your self-giving love has done.

Your goodness and mercy will never fail,
for you take pity on everything frail.
Creation flows with a spontaneous psalm
in praise of your strong tenderness that saves
                              us from ultimate harm.

PALM CROSSES

The air rings with praises.
From the top of its upright trunk
the palm tree raises
a tuft of huge branches:
strong shapes curving in one movement
upwards and outwards,
dark pinnate fronds held high
to celebrate the victory
of grace over self-improvement
as the Servant King rides by.

Then the branches are broken
and hurled down by many hands.
Before the leaves have spoken
of the Lord's peace together
they are seized as if by violent weather:
beaten, strewn, dashed,
their substance torn and slashed.
They sway from side to side—
these palms that have sometimes made
a welcome shade
in which to shelter or abide.

And now we twist dried strips
of palm into the shape of the cross.
The work of our hands equips
us to enter Jerusalem with the Lord.

A cross can also look like a sword.

THIS EARTHLING

This little crumb
that lies in my hand
looking bland,
this insubstantial thing,
this earthling,
light as a petal,
gentle as a snowflake,
soft as a kiss, assails
my composure and makes
my heart ache.
It pierces me like a bitter wind;
it sinks into my flesh
like driven nails.
It is determined
to break my self-regard, and strips
away my façade, touching my lips
like a live coal from the altar.

This fleck,
this speck,
this splinter of the true cross,
weighs on me
like a heavy beam of loss
which Jesus has called me to bear.
How can such a small meal
strengthen me for the task,
and save me from despair?
By looking at Jesus I know the answer,
but the mystery stays,
and I shall ask
the same question all my days.

COSTLY PERFUME

Smell is immediately evocative;
jasmine, camellia, hyacinth and rose
stir the heart when they enter through the nose.
Smell brings back a path, a doorstep, a windowledge, a wall,
and invites us to listen for an approaching footfall.

Memory is ultimately provocative;
a house, a host, hospitality and wine
are more than a symbol and more than a sign.
Memory banishes the stench of death from the tomb,
and incites us to let Christ's costly perfume fill the room.

WHAT CHILD IS THIS?

What child is this
who appears, ancient beyond his days,
whose eyes shine with a terrible joy,
whose heart is ablaze?

What child is this who lies
exposed to the harsh desert wind?
Is it we who have sinned?
Who has rejected him?
What evil has he done?
Will anyone protect him
from the cruel sun?

He makes no sound,
he utters no cry,
but the howls of hyenas surround
the hillside
where he is cast out to die.

God will provide
in the wilderness a way of hope,
a healing passiontide.

The child pleads.
His heart burns and bleeds.
Love flames, flows, consumes and feeds.

CROSSWISE

All things crosswise,
slant, oblique,
all kinds of latticing
and criss-cross trelliswork,
every technique
that you can devise
for shading, such as hatching
and cross-hatching—
these are a screen,
a resistance to light,
invading the gaps, and matching
the shadows that lurk
in the night.

Yet the darkness twines
around small chinks that glow.
There is a flicker
as through wicker.
A slight sheen escapes,
moving to and fro.
Its contrast outlines
unaccountable shapes,
and I begin to see beyond
the random cracks
as the shadows abscond.

The glory of Jesus ransacks
the spaces between heart and mind,
hidden from humankind.
It is at once a fragmented light
and dazzlingly bright.

IS THERE A GOD WHO HEARS?

Lord, you hear the distant rumble of thunder
and the sound of the gasping earth.
You hear the cheep of the fledgling
as the predator stalks it, and the grief
of the mother whose child will never come to birth.
You hear the rustle of the leaves
that have withered in the drought,
and the sigh of the person who is cast out.

All who are cauterized by conflict,
disease and every kind of lack,
all who perpetrate they know not what,
all who have no breath to answer back—
these are like a procession of mourners,
moving with numb hearts and heavy tread
to the sound of a muffled drum:
the dead who bury the dead.

You hear all who are too weary for lamentation,
all whose eyes are too dry for any tears.
You hear the speechless provocation
that calls God to witness when hope disappears:
'Is there any sorrow like our sorrow?
Is there a God who hears?
Who has known grief like the grief we bear,
beyond utterance and beyond prayer?'

On the cross you have offered yourself
to be the voice of all who suffer and die.
Their anguish is your anguish;
their abandonment is your cry.

GOD IS NOT LIKE THIS

What are you to me, Lord God?
To what can I liken you?
In what categories can I find you out?
Where assuage hunger, fear and doubt?
By what notions can I know you?
In what nuances can I see
the shadow of your form?
How can I take your fastness by storm?

Out of clay, out of a sod,
I construct a substance for you.
Out of your creation
I create—oh God—my god.
Every picture is placarded
with a warning shout:
'God is not like this!'
Every word provokes a sharp riposte:
'Cross this cipher out!
Consign it to the abyss!'

You are different
from my highest thoughts.
You are not contained in the profundities
to which my unknowing resorts.

I am nothing; you are everything.
How, then, can I see you
except on the cross, where, in full view
and scandalously free,
you have become nothing like me—
my Lord and my God?

SPRING TIDE

We are an angry sea driven by a gale
of pride and fear, with waves whipped up high
between short-lived furrows,
towers rising in uproar,
heaving to the heavens as if to terrify,
and crashing in fury on the shore.

We do not know our limits.
We are a destructive swell
that surges over fields and villages
in a ruthless invasion that nothing can quell.

Lord, you knew from the beginning
that in us freedom would come to compulsion,
blessing to cursing, love to pain,
that in a stubborn convulsion
the green grass would be submerged
under an expanse of salty grey,
reflecting the foreboding of a stormy day.

Silently, like land swallowed up
under the flood, you are engulfed by sin.
Patiently you wait for the water to subside,
while the fields cry out in anguish
at the death of spring in the fierce spring tide.

In all this devastation you bless
those who curse you, and forgive those who destroy.
In fertile fields wheat will grow
to make bread for all to enjoy,
and from your death a torrent of new life will flow.

THE WISDOM OF THE AGES

Jesus is the wisdom of the ages—
wisdom unafraid and full of delight.
He is newer than the freshness of the morning
and gentler than the enveloping beauty of the night.
Wisdom calls to us with understanding,
never proclaiming itself for its own sake,
but showing forth its being in its doing:
quick to forgive and able to remake.

Wisdom is the heart of God who loves us,
held on the cross from the beginning in pain,
but newly put to death in every age,
and ever rising in radiance to reign.
Wisdom is obedience in a world bent
on seizing supremacy, self-giving, hour by hour,
under a dictatorship that eats its heart
out in a ruthless desire for power.

Wisdom does not push itself forward;
it does not scheme or machinate, but fulfils the law.
It upholds love's pre-eminence, suffering
the disjunction between time and eternity to restore
all things, steadfast in kindness and strong to endure.
Wisdom transforms every moment into pure
joy, bringing to completion, through falsehood
and the agony of evil, its purposes of good.

GRACE

I speak
of God's grace—
what else is there
to speak of?
What else
could take its place?
Everything else
is an absence,
an emptiness, a space.

Grace is God's gift
for everyone everywhere,
as free as fresh air,
like water overflowing
with plenty to spare,
a new garment to wear.
Grace is love
that fills
the whole earth
with its flair.
Grace on the cross
is God's heart laid bare.

A BLOOD-RED BEAD

Jesus came
to one small place.
He came like a single
precious seed,
a new variety
never before found,
a windflower of grace
that would abound.
A blood-red bead
the colour of a sunset,
like a ruby
in a king's ring,
or like the sweat
and the anguished cry
of one about to die,
was sown in spring.
It was grown
to dedicate
a garden of great
worth, to fill
it with colour and scent,
to make it spill
over with loving intent
throughout the year.
Now its glory, shown
openly at last,
is sown broadcast
across every frontier.

PEACE

Nowadays calm is all the rage,
and, like a lion in a cage,
we pace up and down with clenched fist
to find a freedom that does not exist.
Or, like a lamb grazing in a field,
we approach a death to which we cannot yield.
But peace—the word is an evangelist.
Peace is known in tumult; peace is deep,
as when, tossed by the storm
on the lake, Jesus first lay asleep,
then showed his power to transform
the chaos. 'Peace be with you,' Jesus said,
after he had risen from the dead.
Peace is his gift, through his passion.
It was not something he could easily fashion
or the healing would have been too slight,
the cure too weak to reach the spite.
So peace has come through bloody warfare,
and his willing entry into despair.
In his freedom to act the lion roars
and the lamb is struck by the lion's paws.
Jesus never spoke of calm
which is a superficial balm.
Peace is richer, finer, far;
it withstands the assault and heals the scar.
We are in the fire but passing through it;
there is grief in the heart, but, construe it
as we may, the joy is in the pain,
for the lamb's peace is in the lion's mane.

A DOUBLE-BLIND TRIAL

'What is God like?' is a question
to which answers multiply.
If you follow the suggestion
that faith can testify,
before you say 'Amen to that'
take heed of the caveat:
we live in a double bind.

Faith can provide
no certainty on either side,
and, since from the beginning
the faithful have never stopped sinning,
it is the blind who lead the blind.

What is certain is that while we wait
for something more reliable
to make life viable,
the time is getting late.

Call the cross a double-blind trial,
and our denial
only goes to show
that, at a cost we cannot know,
God's grace will always flow.

His faithfulness gives him away,
and enables us to say
again and again:
'Amen. Amen.'

ONE MOMENT

Was there
ever
a time when
a culture
of blame
did not exist,
since
Adam blamed
Eve
and Eve blamed
the serpent
and the serpent
hissed?

There was
just
one
moment
when truth
and mercy
kissed.

RUNNING FREE

Like a ship's master
who remains resolute
as he sails a perilous route
far from any land,
with a hoard
of treasure on board
that puts at risk every hand,
Christ rides his cross
over the wide sea.
The tall waves overreach
the small ship
as the storms rip,
yet he stays,
bound by love to the masthead,
running free,
while menace rises
from the seabed,
and the mast sways
like a stricken tree.

God is our native land
where every cabined heart
will expand in open space
on a shining strand.
This voyage will end
in the harbour never before
visited, but known in part,
and talked about
as the birthplace
from which everyone living
is eager to set out.

ON THE WAY

Lord, you are with us on the way,
walking beside us, talking
to us and listening to what we say.

I know the lie of the land
like a face intently scanned:
the dust that thickens the air,
the rocks that blankly stare,
the arid hills,
the battle of wills,
the stubborn toss
of the head, the harsh crack
that appears like a cross
in the familiar track.

The sun sinks fast.
It is the irrevocable past
that drags us down.
Yet, without a frown,
you teach us to see
that your crucified and risen glory
can transform our story
and set us free.

Lord, don't go on ahead;
stay with us and break bread.

THE KINGFISHER

Lord, to love at all
is to embrace pain,
for love is a gift
difficult to retain.
It is love that makes
us cry,
and love for our sakes
that made you die.

You have poured out
your Spirit like pure rain—
a well-wisher
that fills rivers
and makes a good habitat
for all they can contain.
Now we see a flash,
a bright splash
of sapphire: a kingfisher,
once banished
by pollution.
We thought its beauty
had vanished
for ever from our sight,
but now it rises
with feathers alight
in a glad restitution.

Such love as yours, Lord,
nothing could destroy.
You give yourself constantly,
and so we live with Easter joy.

A SCULPTOR

Lord, if failure has pursued me
and overtaken me, if my way is empty
and I cannot lift myself up
with heartstrings of clay,
if I am weary of my lot,
if, when I try to run,
I am rooted to the spot,
if my life is a sham—
I will tell you who I think I am.

Then, like a sculptor who reveals
an enchanting form hidden in stone,
you will show me how it is with you,
and who I really am—as yet unknown.

By the action of hammer and chisel
and the skill of his hand,
a sculptor can create out of granite
a figure that will withstand
dread. His imagination can trace
reality faithfully and innovate
design to reveal life and grace
of movement, with supple limbs
released from all that dead weight.

You will create in me a new heart,
flexible and festive in all its ways—
a life that dances in the steps
of its maker, that holds your gaze
and delights in the love of its healer
with swift and joyful praise.

SEEDS

I pour a few specks into my hand
to sow in the flowerbed.
They are lighter than grains of sand,
and as gritty
as crumbs of dry bread.
I am filled with pity
for such inconsequential pieces
that lie almost hidden in the creases
of my open palm;
I cannot keep them from harm.
Their dull brown and black
could disappear through the crack
between finger and thumb.
I try to scatter them, but they cling
to my sweat like a ring
of hard-water scum.

The seeds fall to the ground
at last to be buried and then unbound.
I hold in these dead particles the hope
that, under sunshine and soft showers,
something better than paper flowers
will grow along this slope—
not a picture printed on a packet,
capturing last year's story
in the perfection of a borrowed jacket,
but the promise of unknown glory:
living colour, symmetry and scent,
given not lent.

RESTORED

We went up river against the tidal current,
our arms aching, each pulling on an oar.
We came back resting the oars in the rowlocks,
the flow of the river carrying us towards the shore.

We went out in thick darkness, picking our way
along the unforgiving roughness of the path.
We came back lit by the strong beam of a lantern,
and the memory of songs around a welcoming hearth.

We went out sadly, mourning our unfaithfulness,
wondering that the very things we love we forsake.
We came back rejoicing with singing and dancing,
celebrating God's power to heal and remake.

We went out in weakness, swaying and staggering,
our lips parched, our eyes staring, unseeing, ahead.
We came back strengthened, like people who have feasted,
like people whom God has raised from the dead.

FAITH AND DOUBT

Yes, sometimes I doubt—
isn't that what faith is about?
Faith isn't certainty, so we can rule that out.

Faith is holding together what is revealed
and what is hidden.
It's head in a fragrant field
and feet in a midden.
It's losing your footing on an ascent
and free-falling by experiment.
It's plunging into the deepest night
and rising to see everything in a new light.

There's no scientific proof
that will establish faith once for all,
but, if we don't keep ourselves aloof,
it doesn't fail to enthral.
Moreover, faith can no more be disproved
than mountains can be moved.

Faith is God's gift, given for the asking;
no one is given short shrift
who desires an unmasking.
Faith is knowing and not knowing;
receiving and owing.
It implies no merit,
but speaks of an enigmatic kingdom to inherit.

Through faith I believe that God takes our part,
and that Jesus Christ, crucified and risen,
reveals the grace of God's heart.

SUMMER

THE MERCY OF GOD

Oh, the mercy of God,
how it creates and redeems!
Feather and fountain and flower
and elusive hour—
everything seems
transformed, everything gleams.
How mercy refreshes!

As a willow grows
it enmeshes
its branches against the sky,
and sends
its roots down deep
where the moisture flows
from the river's sweep,
or else it will die.

So our life depends
on mercy, which is the spaciousness
of the air
and the solidity of the earth for us,
and water's graciousness.

'Lord have mercy,' is our prayer,
and God, who held out his hands
over us all,
answers us before we call
because he understands.

A REDEEMED LANDSCAPE

Lord, you will never separate
yourself from the earth
which is yours by birth,
by your death and rising,
and by your sympathizing
with our weakness.

Though we see bleakness,
your constant love is deep
within all that you have made.
You sustain and keep
a redeemed landscape
where everything bears
your name inscribed and inlaid.
Only your obedience
can willingly transcend
the limitations of our hearts
like a shining friend.

Your coming chases
us from our resting places,
as when particles of dust
that have drifted
across a path are lifted
and blown by the wind.
But you transform us,
your love and mercy stream
towards us, and we are raised
like dust in a sunbeam
that is almost sequinned
and dances with a gleam.

A MARBLE

Lord, of itself
the world is not
solid enough;
it is such
ephemeral stuff.
Like a marble
in a child's hand
it could so easily be lost
in the sand,
fretfully tossed
aside to roll away,
never to see the light
of another day.
It is your reality
that gives it meaning,
your love that redeems
it from futility,
your glory that streams
through it, your care
that sustains,
your peace that reigns
over it, your prayer
that intercedes
for it, your body
that feeds
its life, your Spirit
dwelling within it
to strengthen and fill
that will bring it
at last
with all creation
to do your will.

A NEW SHARED LANGUAGE

There is a world of silence as dead
as fields from which life has fled.
Those confined within it do not know
the first cry of a child,
or whether the falling snow
whispers to creatures in the wild.
They cannot hear the breaking wave,
the melody of laughter,
the hollow sound of a voice in a cave
or the echoes that follow after.
But they have learnt a new shared
language of vibrant expression,
gesture, response and intercession.

The glory of Jesus has declared
a dynamic movement of grace
in which flesh hears and understands
the animation of the face
and the flow of signs made by hands.
The silent music of this choir
is made by tongues of fire
with sparks leaping from heart
to heart, through interactive art,
as his embodied truth appears.

God's creative Spirit opens deaf ears
to the theme of the cross that heals
confusion. His free Spirit unseals
the voice of the dumb so that it sings
of the unity of all things
and the joy that unfettered love brings.

HOLY CONNECTIONS

Love is the greatest blessing
of all. It is not possessing
another, but self-giving
for the joy of living.
There is a web of silk intertwined,
a mesh of hearts combined,
a net first cast into the sea
by fishermen's hands.
Love forms delicate bands
of silver filigree
which do not imprison but set free.
These are holy connections,
despite our imperfections.
Love makes a fabric stitched
with flowers and enriched
with mirrors to reflect a smile
and multiply laughter.
Love is accepting in style,
and peace comes after.

HOW LOVELY IT IS

So we must love one another—
not a conclusion
but a continual new beginning,
since we live in confusion
and no one stops sinning.
Even at our most well-meaning
we can seem overweening,
and there are hard landings,
broken words and misunderstandings.

So we must love one another—
a heartfelt plea,
for we are all in debt
to unity. How lovely it is to set
each other completely free
in the forgiveness of Jesus our Lord,
who can heal the unkindest blow,
so that amongst us his peace may flow.
It is like a softly stippled
sky, promising fair weather,
or like the gently rippled
disturbance on the surface of a lake,
marked by a breeze at daybreak
as if by the barbs of a feather.

Love cannot be stored.
Nothing is more precious to give
and more joyful to receive;
nothing helps us as much to believe
that there is no other way to live.

FORGIVENESS

Forgiveness is the hardest thing
to conceive,
and harder still to achieve.

It is as delicate as a lacewing,
buffeted by the wind,
transparent and thin-skinned.
It is as strong
as a limpet's life-long
hold on a rock
to withstand the shock
of the waves that form
and break in the storm.

Does fraud
deserve the mercy of the Lord?
Does pride
open his arms wide?
No, but nothing can diminish
his love. At any cost he will finish
what he has made.
We heap blame upon blame,
but his reply is always the same:
'Don't be afraid.'
To the prisoner he brings release,
to the sinner grace and peace.
To all people on earth
his love gives true worth.

And then, between us who sin,
to and fro forgiveness can begin.

ONE COMMON LIFE

Can a butterfly enter the chrysalis
again? Can a bird on the wing
forget to sing,
fold its head on its breast
and enter the egg in the nest?

No, but Jesus has entered the tomb,
changing it into a room
from which new life has burst.
Now our worst
dread is displayed
and we are no longer afraid,
for there will always be
witnesses to the breaking
of death's bonds and our remaking.

Can continents and islands drift
back into a single mass of land
in a worldwide shift?
Can bread that is broken
come together to make one loaf
when the word is spoken?

No, but God can create,
from many broken pieces,
one race and one common life
that flourishes and increases.
He can make one community
to sing with one heart and one voice
of the love that is always
faithful, and to rejoice.

PEOPLE OF MANY NATIONS

Once we were like random points
outside a circle without pattern
or relationship or design,
but Jesus has drawn us
into the meaning of his love
through his cruciform sign.
Now we are like petals arranged
around the centre of a sunflower,
close enough to touch and unite.
We are like the crystal droplets
of a chandelier placed around a light.
We are like a flotilla of small boats
celebrating the joyful presence
of the mother ship and its goodwill.
We are like houses, built of disparate
materials in many architectural styles,
clustered around a cathedral on a hill.
We are people of many nations gathered
into one community of thanksgiving
to praise one holy name.

Jesus is with us like a fine tree
that grows vigorously in a garden;
he has planted eternal life in our midst,
and this is the salvation we proclaim.

We are still the same—truants,
deserters, fugitives, renegades—
but he will bring us all to the completion
of the love for which he came.

HIGHLIGHTING

The Spirit of Jesus
has the disconcerting knack
of exploding
with a rattle and a crack
like a jumping jack
in a surprise attack
that overtakes me
by zig-zagging under my feet
from behind my back.

The Spirit
is also like a steady flame
lit to proclaim
a victory which has left
nothing the same.
He quietens
my desire for fame
by highlighting
the reason why Jesus came,
and illuminating
in lambent red and gold
the glory of his name.

A CHANGE OF DIRECTION

Lord, teach me the reality
of your cross. Turn
me round to face
you, crucified one,
you whose grace
I cannot escape.
Make me willing to learn
from the chance events
that you shape.

Open my eyes to see you
and my heart to know
you in that place where my sin
holds you and your love
holds me and will always flow.

Let the sin that drives me
from you quickly draw me back
to the mercy I cannot ignore.
Let me be like the waves
that rush to break
against the upward
slope of the shore.
They surge and throw
up shingle and wrack
at their furthest range,
only to pause and make
a swirling change
of direction. Then, pulled free
by gravity, they go
smoothly down into the sea.

THE CROSSWIND

The kingdom of God is like a seascape,
constantly changing its colour and shape.

The wind is fresh and the clouds are chasing
across the sky. A herring gull glides, racing

the downward rush, tilting and airlifting
over the white-flecked waves, spindrifting,

bracing its frail body against the crosswind
whose power to disturb us God will never rescind.

A BEACHCOMBER

We are like misshapen pieces of wood:
a stealthy configuration
floating under a limitless moon,
or ambushed by a tide that washes
against the edge of the noon.

We spend ourselves in fruitless labour
which our own hearts oppose.
There is neither profit nor pleasure,
neither relish nor leisure,
amongst the detritus of the shallows.
Whilst our lives form and re-form
our cry is: 'Useless! Useless!'
Like the seagull's lament,
it competes for a hearing
with the waves, the veering
west wind and the storm.

But Jesus is a beachcomber.
He walks where sand and water mingle,
retrieving flotsam from the eddying foam.
He bends down low to take
jetsam from the shingle,
knowing what it will signify,
looking at it with an artist's eye,
holding it in his hands and taking it home.

Whatever he saves from the ravage
of the pitiless ebb and flow
and the savage assault of the sea
he transforms into something carefree.

A DEEP-SEA DIVER

We are like sunken vessels.
We have struck the rocks
like someone who wrestles
with God, and their sharpness
has pierced our sides
with a sickening crack.
We are holed beneath the surface.
We lie where barnacles stack,
shrouded in purple laver
and bladderwrack.

But Jesus has descended,
like a deep-sea diver,
into the ocean's night.
He has salvaged the wrecks,
raising us into the welcoming light.

He has rightly assessed
the damage of the storm blast.
He has stripped from their holdfast
the leathery strands that entangled
us. He has ripped away the fronds
that choked and strangled
us in their unrelenting bonds.

Now, in the harbour where the gulls
wheel and cry, the wind blows
without force but without abating.
Lively vessels are waiting
ready to set sail in good heart.
The voyage is about to start.

A BEACON

Jesus has lit a beacon
on a remote headland
that hangs over the sea.
The fire is hidden at first,
and seems to weaken—
seems almost to stop—
licking quietly at the wood
that forms the inner
structure. Then hand over hand
smoke climbs, curling
over the logs. Sparks burst
into the sky and airdrop.
Flames below break free
and recruit
dazzling flames that shoot
upwards, leaving a mark
of radiance in the eyes.
They gain strength and rise,
wildly, eagerly hurling
themselves against the dark,
which has not withstood
the conflagration.
The brilliance of the flare
reaches high
across sea and sky
to celebrate and declare
God's salvation.

THE HOLIDAY

Lord,
when you restored
us we moved to a new
rhythm and enjoyed the wide view
with all our strength.
The route was beyond our usual length,
but we stepped easily that day
because it seemed
that everything was redeemed
by your glory. The landscape lay
open to the kindness of your light,
and we rejoiced at the transparency of the sight.

Dune, salting, marsh,
mudflat and reedbed make a harsh
habitat in winter's grip,
but after spring's courtship
they were alive
with birds that thrive
in the lull
between gale and storm.
Heron, oyster catcher, gull,
marsh harrier and avocet
were glad to glide
and pirouette
in the warm
air. Through earth, sky and tide
our hearts you simplified.

When we took our rest
we were like children blessed.

A FISH OUT OF WATER

Lord, I am like a fish
out of water, caught in a net
but too small to keep yet.
I lie at the water's edge,
so near and yet so far
from my heart's desire,
lashing fitfully, gasping feebly,
about to expire.

The sea is my saving element.
If I could once more
live in the freedom
of that softly pearled
three-dimensional world
I should flow with the current
and follow the tide,
where floating is natural
and to swim is to glide,
and every streamlined
movement in your sight
is beautifully clothed
with the glimmer
of unfathomable light.

Lord, you were the friend
of fishermen. You stood
by the lake and at your command
they caught a great quantity
of fish. Only throw
me back into the water, send
me deep, and I shall grow.

A SUNBURST

Faith is one of God's gifts:
through faith he lifts
our hearts to him
lest our eyes become dim,
lest we sink and sigh,
oppressed by evil under every pseudonym,
and sicken and die.

And he gives us another gift
that brings about a shift
in our perception: hope,
so that, though we stumble and grope
in the dark, because he suffered our worst,
we are like pieces shaken in a kaleidoscope,
and our lives are lit by the symmetry of a rising sunburst.

HIDE AND SEEK

Lord, you hide and I seek—
and the silence is bleak.
I count to a hundred or more,
and I am still in two minds about you.
I open my eyes, unsure
whether to look for you
or to leave you out and withdraw,
because you are a troublemaker,
a boneshaker,
with an unpredictable streak.

You seek and I hide—
and it is a kind of suicide.
I am in darkness, detached and alone.
I plot a disguise;
I agonize.
But when you find me
you set me free,
and my defences are overthrown
by the love that moved the stone.

You are nearer to me than my own face
and as hidden from my eyes,
yet I see your grace.

LIGHT FROM LIGHT

When particles of dust appear as boulders,
when grasses appear as giant ferns
invading the skies with angled shoulders,
when the crumpled petals of a poppy
unfold to make an ocean of blood,
dark at the centre like the black mud
of conflagration and catastrophic storms—
then I wonder where God is
in these spreading and enlarging forms?

I have searched the empty spaces
between the boulders, and forced my way
painfully into cavities that convey
nameless fears, where vague shadows hide.
I have seen ferns with fronds
that multiply, crotch upon crotch,
fractals that increase to obscure knowledge,
serpents' tongues that dart and divide
light from light as I watch.

I have looked long into the contrast
at the heart of a poppy, till,
accepting the darkness at last,
the judgement heals and purifies.
I close my eyes. On the blank screen
of the retina, the fiery red turns to green,
and the black blotch is a bright swatch
of resurgent light, unforeseen.

A ROBIN

As I kneel by the flowerbed
and loosen the soil
so that the roots can spread,
a robin hops
right up to my fingers.
My digging stops
and yet he lingers.
I feel honoured by this exquisite
bird's visit.
His eye is as bright as tinfoil,
his back is brown like the earth,
but his red breast
is like the dying sun in the west.
I keep very still.
I remember that I have heard
his brilliant trill,
full of light and mirth,
and I have seen him flying
over the hedge.
Now I can almost touch
him, but he is such
a friend, and he is undeterred.

You come closer to me, Lord,
than the bird that I can see.
You are with me
like the ultrasound
of a wing that has soared
unseen, but is known and found
at my mind's quiet edge.

A PEREGRINE FALCON

Lord, you are like a peregrine falcon,
led out to wait in the morning mist.
Silent and still, under control,
it perches on the falconer's wrist,
as if, in the open country,
it had chosen to alight on a pole.
It is no stranger to captivity.
Its nature is to work while it is day,
but a blinding hood covers its head,
and in its humiliation and dread
deep darkness envelops its soul.
Then the hood is removed.
In a burst of light its wings beat fast
and it rises into the air, swooping past,
majestically free. Now its flight
is a flash of feathers, black and white,
swift and strong through the fields.
It glides silently, as its body yields
to the air, and drops, gripping its prey.

By what right does it act with such skill?
Who has given it authority to kill?
Those golden claws are red with the stain
of some poor creature that was slain,
and the hooked beak looks cruel.

                    Lord, you alone
have power over the life and death of what is your own.
Is anyone safe from the inevitability of your call?
I am in your hands. Only give me a pilgrim's
faith, and be with me at nightfall.

OUT ON A LIMB

Let silence clothe me inside and outside.
When I wait in silence, when no words fall
from my lips, when my song is under my breath
and my prayer is under my heart, then all
the space that opens around me discloses Jesus.
To be silent is to be out on a limb, to trust
myself to the root and branch of the tree.
Silence discloses me to myself: dust to dust.
When I hear the emptiness of my heart
which I have tried to fill, in my need,
with stolen goods, I hear also Jesus
telling me that I cannot possibly succeed,
and promising the love for which I plead:
'Make haste and come down straight away,
for I must stay at your house today.'

THE FELLING OF A TREE

A felled tree crashes to the ground
and is stripped of its branches
which are chopped for firewood to give
warmth and light. The wood blanches,
it is consumed, but nothing is taken away.
Everything original, all its store of energy,
is transformed by interchange and interplay.

The felling of a tree distresses me.
I mourn its grandeur, its uprightness,
its awesome height brought low so fast.
When it comes down, it lies on the ground
like a tower demolished, or a broken mast.
It reminds me of storm damage after a drought,
or the stillness of a body laid out.

Whether I shall serve God better alive
or dead I do not know, but these things
I observe, ponder and admire:
a horizontal tree is home in its turn
to a commonwealth of creatures that feed
on its goodness. Green wood will not burn,
but dry wood kindles well and makes a good fire.

The commandments of Jesus are not for self-preservation.
We are his body, our common life is his gift,
and he has commanded us to lay ourselves out
for the life of the world in a radical shift.

HOSPITALITY

Jesus has invited us to come into a room
where everyone is welcome as his guest.
Better an almshouse where compassion is
than a castle which will be repossessed.

The open door is hospitality, the walls
are freedom and the ceiling is praise.
The floor is the bedrock of his truth,
and the windows let in heaven's rays.

On the walls he has hung bright handmade
tapestries whose colours will never fade.
Flowers and rich fruits pierce the shadows,
every leaf has found its place, and every blade

of grass springs up with shining artistry.
There are creatures skilfully sewn to trace
a framework where serpents, wolves, whales
and crowing cocks are portrayed with grace.

The scene is alive with a great crowd
of people from all nations: young and old,
singing with joy as they worship
the lamb impaled in a circle of gold.

The room supports a table spread with a fair
white cloth for a meal that signifies love.
Outside lies a garden, carefully tended,
and from a tree comes the gentle sound of a dove.

AUTUMN

EIGHT GOLDFINCHES

This afternoon
there were eight goldfinches
within inches
of my window, like a string of beads
on the lavender seeds
that I had forgotten to prune.
They made the dead stems
shine like precious gems,
with a flash
of yellow under the wing, a splash
of red round the beak,
and a streak
of black like a widow's peak,
on the head.

Now they feast,
but how will they fare
when the bushes are bare
and the wind comes from the north-east?

In my heart the glory of that yellow
will never mellow,
nor will the joy of that red
fail to spread,
nor will the tautness of that black
become slack.

And this is God's unfathomable art:
he who knows me through and through
will keep my life in his heart
and make it come true.

SOLID PRAYER

When I was a child
I used to thank God for a mild
climate without extremes
of drought or tempest.
In my dreams
there was always a harvest
of plenty, maximum yields
gathered from easy fields
and gardens, crowned with a bright
halo of holy light.
Now I am glad our harvest meal
is a modest appeal
to remember all who hunger and thirst.

Lord, teach us to put first
the poor whose part you always take.
You ache
to see justice done
for everyone.
Teach us to share
what is no more our own than the air.
Teach us to offer solid prayer.

HARVEST FESTIVAL

A hundred harvests go to waste,
blighted by commercial haste.
In the forests the trees stand bare,
like the ghosts of an industrial past,
victims of a poisonous blast
that still pollutes the air.
Creation, in labour with a stillborn child,
groans with grief and is reviled
for the desolation of a deadly birth.
Silent and stricken is the earth,
and sick the people who, through greed,
have bound the hope that Jesus freed.

There is a garden where everything grows
well. Here a cool river always flows,
and corn produces seed a hundredfold.
Here to love is to have and to hold.
Peace and plenty, like a blessing, rain down
mercy, and set on every head a crown.
Our cup runs over with fine wine,
and the bread we eat is a healing sign.
Here joy and laughter are the reapers,
and people are each other's keepers.

RICH AND POOR

The rich–poor divide—
how it unsettles our pride,
and God is not on our side.
His is an upside down economy
with a bias against autonomy.
So the hungry, the poor,
the excluded—they are blessed,
while those who fill their store
with the things they love best
suffer a revolutionary blow:
they accumulate nothing but woe.

And I know what I'm talking about,
for, between a whisper and a shout,
this message hasn't left me out.
Wealth is the power to choose
and the freedom to misuse.
All or nothing might bring ease;
it's these half measures that tease.
How to balance on a quivering tight rope?
How to keep my footing on a slope?
How to descend into the bottomless pit
without losing sight of the exit?

The words of Jesus are intended to shock,
to blast my heart from its false bedrock.

PRIESTS OF THE EARTH

Lord, you have made us
priests of the earth,
but we have devoured your gift
and dimmed your light.
You gave us the fruits
of care and communion,
but we have been swift
to strip bare every tree in sight.
You gave the wheat to ripen,
but, like people who sleepwalk,
we have eaten the seed-corn
while it was still on the stalk.
We build barns and store up goods
for our own satisfaction;
we hide our gains in strongholds
as a distraction.
But we have forgotten the maggot
in the apple, the blight on the rose
and the questions you pose.
Everything we seize is infected
by scab, rust, gall and spot;
everything we hoard is spoilt
by mould and rot.

True priests represent you
to your people and your people to you;
true priests re-present
your sacrificial love in the work they do.
Their hands take, bless and give.
They sing creation's praise to your glory
and so learn generously to live.

ONE OUT OF TEN

One out of ten;
it is the same now as then.
One leper praised God and knelt
to thank Jesus for the healing he felt.

The other nine
who did not see healing as a sign
of their salvation, but went away—
where on earth are they?

A tenth, a tithe,
set aside by hand or scythe,
has always been God's allotted portion,
representing thanksgiving hedged with caution.

Yet the smallest piece of bread
can give life to the dead,
and a little wine in a cup
can consecrate all creation and raise it up.

BY DEFAULT

Lord, it isn't fair:
poverty depends on how you compare
yourself with others, and so does wealth.
Your standards endanger my health.

Your demands are unrealistic—
altogether too idealistic.
Is it any mistake of mine
if I can't allow divine
distortion
to affect my small portion?

Over the years
I've learnt to close my ears
to the outrageous things you say,
to look down and turn away.

And I'm still trying to escape by default
from your assault.

BEGGARS AT HOME

If it is true that Jesus welcomes all,
even outcasts and sinners, to eat
with him, who would presume to forestall
the Lord who takes the lowest seat?
Who would dare to limit love,
claiming authority from above,
or who, in the name of good order,
would act as grace's hoarder?
In this company no one is turned away,
for all are regarded as bona fide,
so there is no need for mirror or mask,
and all receive before they ask.
There is no fashionable gastronome,
no condescension from top table,
but beggars who are at home
in the simplicity of a stable.
They have learned their table manners
from the Lord to whom they sing hosannas.
They love and honour him so much
because he has reached out to touch
them with good news: they are forgiven.
Their lives are no longer driven
by lust for power or pride of place;
instead they are freely welcomed by overflowing grace.

OUR HUMANITY

We are scattered like dry bones.
We are carried away like branches
broken off by vandals.
We are like empty snails' shells
that have been crushed
underfoot, dislodged stones
that rattle over a ledge
from a cairn in the fells,
discarded packets that lie crumpled,
that everyone disowns.

We have become as insubstantial
as dust that matters not a jot.
We inhabit each a deserted room,
a hollow grave, a vacant lot.

Like people who have been captured
by a contemptuous enemy and receive
treatment that takes a bitter toll,
we long for deliverance and rest.
We dream of food for body and soul.

Lord, have mercy on our weakness,
and give us the bread that restores.
Fill us with your awakening Spirit,
for our humanity is made glorious in yours.

AT A LOSS

O you who are fire and flood within me,
you who blaze in my heart and flow
through my bones—how can I keep you
within bounds, you who take no
account of moderation or propriety?
Am I to reduce you to the size
of a crumb so that I can swallow you
and see you vanish before my eyes?
Am I to speak of you in a sentence
that will become mist like breath on a cold
morning as soon as it leaves my mouth?
Why have you taken up your freehold
abode in my weak frame? Your enterprises
search me and find me at a loss.
I asked for your comforting presence
but you have never stopped shattering
my peace with the turbulence of your wings.
I sought shelter but you have exposed me.
I looked for love, but your justice brings
love through cost, conflict and a cross.
I longed for life, but every day you take my breath,
confronting me with the life that comes through death.

I have no God but the one who comes to me in
                                    bread and wine,
and holds me in his own hands in this sign.

ANGELS' COSTUMES

I would like a job designing
angels' costumes—or whatever streamlining
we use to picture them and make-believe
they have a function which is valid.
I would not have them wan or pallid,
pasty creatures that float and waft
at shoulder height, wings held aloft,
painful to look at, smugly naive.
I would employ strong colours for bold
beings: scarlet, cerise, gold,
shocking pink, crimson, magenta.
These angels have no impedimenta;
they move like flames leaping,
like fiery fountains scorching and sweeping
heaven's horizons with exuberant grace
that emblazons God's nature in endless space.

What are these incendiary dancers?
We ask questions and debate the answers.

I have never seen an angel,
but I have seen God's message in a glistening shell,
and in a scarlet pimpernel
whose petals close when the sky is overcast.
God's colours cannot be surpassed.
He will not leave us dull and dreary,
defeated by a discredited theory.
He will give us his own attire:
his steadfast love and his cleansing fire.

ALL SAINTS'

All Saints'
falls
when nature paints
in bold
a pavilion of trees
hung with squalls
of amber, russet, gold
and vermilion. Seas
of wine red
reflect a sadness
in the gladness,
as if a cosmic wound bled
with overspill.
The wooded hill
is decked in festival style,
but the air grieves
for the endgame
of the falling leaves,
and for their fragile,
trembling hold
on life that will turn
to mould.
The footpaths burn,
the ground
where we have trod
is on fire,
and every mound
is a funeral pyre
where tongues of flame
shout: 'Glory to God!'

SMALL PEOPLE

All
saints are sinners;
they are not people
who have clutched at goodness.
They are small
people who walk tall,
people who continually fall,
sinners touched by the glory
of God's forgiveness and his call.

All
saints belong to Jesus
whom they trusted to transform
their lives. They are his haul
of fish, the harvest
of his trawl
in the dark depths of the sea,
the fruit of his passionate plea:
'Father forgive,'
at the height of the storm.

We are never alone,
for the great company of heaven—
saints known and unknown—
are as near to us in Jesus
as the unborn child is to the caul,
as the corpse is to the pall,
as Jesus is to us
all.

TO LIVE IS TO DIE

Lord, have mercy on this sinner or beginner-saint.
I will not paint
too clear a picture of what is in my heart—
it is enough to start
by saying that I do not want to die.
Nothing will buy
my agreement to such a brutal sacking
or hijacking
of every long-held hope and cherished plan
for my lifespan.
As soon as a child is born into the world, one thing
has the sharpest sting:
before the child can understand what makes it cry
it finds that to live is to die.
This is my complaint: creation needs a new design,
everlasting and benign.
The strange thing is that you have shown
how you have made us your own—
how, through the very death that we so hate
for ourselves, you recreate.
Nevertheless, for me there is a long way to go
before death is more friend than foe.
I am like a bud appearing late, damaged by frost,
withering and soon to be lost.
I praise you for all the saints, known and unknown,
in whom your life is full-blown.

THE LEAVES ARE TURNING

Since, Lord, we shall come to dust
we must learn to trust.

Whether we die young or old
our goods will be sold

or handed over or taken away
and left to decay.

In the first frosts the rowan leaves are turning
crimson. The berries are burning

holes in the sky, making the embers of a brazier
glow for some kind of euthanasia.

Like the feathers of a sick bird the leaves will fall
and lie cold against the stone wall.

But even as the heart groans and grieves
the branches bear new buds for new leaves.

The seasons are a cycle of life and death,
but for us one day—no more breath.

While you give me life I will praise
you and trust in your power to raise.

It is no easy matter—this new living:
it is all dying, burning, scattering and self-giving.

HERE AND NOW

God's kingdom
is here and now.
It is not set apart
from earth in time
or space—
an impossible vow,
a fading chime,
a sidelong glance
at some far distant,
futuristic dance.
It is a pressing
new start,
a change of heart,
a glimpse of God's reality
and his grace,
clothed in the blessing
of materiality.
It flourishes when
rapacious living
and thieving
become giving
and receiving.
God's kingdom is love
that will never cease,
justice and peace,
perfect well-being.
It is creative seeing
that makes an invisible mend
binding the worn threads
and torn shreds
at the earth's fraying end.

THE SHEEP AND THE GOATS

What's wrong with goats,
I should like to know?
Is it something to do with their coats
which are less white than snow
with the texture of tow,
though soft on the under-belly?
Goats are smelly
and shaggy,
but they're sure-footed where it's craggy.

Why are sheep always commended?
Isn't it time their smugness was ended?

I'm pleading
for equality before the law—
or, rather, for a level base
under grace.

A sheep of good breeding
is a natural herbivore,
but someone of the highest class,
who refused to repent,
also ate grass—
a sorry experiment.
Sheep err and stray
when they prefer their own way,
and think that because of their behaviour
they have no need of a Saviour.

Pride comes before a fall—
God help us all.

GOD KNOWS

'Don't be found out!'
is the commandment which you mustn't flout.
Whatever you've done or left undone,
don't be the one
they talk about.

Whether or not the ten are eroded,
the eleventh commandment is never outmoded.
The ten frustrate us all our days
and are calculated to confound our ways,
but the eleventh is cleverly coded
to ensure that we aren't overloaded—
and everyone obeys.

God knows
how easily we suppose
that he can't see what we don't disclose.

St Augustine stood morality on its head:
'Love God and do what you like,' he said.

REMEMBERING

I remember,
this damp, grey November,
a field of poppies in June,
appearing like a hot rash,
splashing their brilliant red
across the countryside that afternoon
like a sea of blood,
a suffering, anguished flood,
gashing the soft green of the young corn,
marking the mind, like a photoflash,
with an image of the war dead
whom we mourn.

Oh, the lamentation of war,
its destructive law,
and the lashing of its blind
fury! And afterwards the grief,
and the honoured names engraved or carved in relief.

Now, as I sit and watch
the rain falling
like the tears I am recalling,
Lord, help my unbelief.

THE KERNEL

You are God
of the one lost sheep, the one fine pearl,
the single hair that falls from the head,
the one tree leaning against the skyline,
the one broken body by which we are fed.

You are God
of every small, holy, hidden thing:
the pinpoint of the individual cell
before it divides with pulsating energy,
the unique kernel of promise in a nutshell.

You are God
of the one particular time and place
by which all times and places are blessed.
Yours is the intimate, personal touch
that draws us into the one lifelong quest.

A FRIEND

Lord, you are a king under a purple cloak,
suffering under the cruelty of a crushing yoke.

Your cross is still your ignominious throne
where the glory of your steadfast love is shown.

Even under duress you did not refuse
the title forced upon you by the bruise

of sin and wickedness. But there's a word
that this generation has preferred.

You said yourself: 'I call you friends.'
That is a generous word which mends

a world of hatred and contempt, and sings
of the grace that holds all things.

A king may rule gloriously, loving and giving,
but a friend is with us in the contingency of living.

WINTER

A HYMN OF PRAISE

A hymn of praise
is an act of love in the dark,
and its power to raise
is like the freedom of the lark.
From a small brown bird,
as invisible on the ground
as sticks for kindling
when the days are dwindling,
a fountain of sparkling sound
is suddenly heard.
Its song is a flight of joy rising high
beyond the sight of the naked eye,
and pouring out across the summer sky.

The bird sings again in dull November
when I remember
the bliss its song expressed
and how it made God's glory manifest.

In the same way
the music of God's grace
will play and replay
in every time and place.

Quietly the Saviour came
to set his rising flame
of passion over the cold earth,
forever bringing to birth,
in our hearts that were undone,
praise for the salvation he has won.

A CANDLE

At the top sways
a flame
like the petal
of a flower. It plays
a glancing game,
trembling a little,
moving with the grace
of acquittal
to partner the darkness
in this place.

Below stands a stick
of white wax
with a pale starkness,
a stem firmly rooted
in the grasp
of gravity, held in metal
claws that clasp,
yet ready to relax
and melt to fuel the wick
until the plant has fruited.

Sometimes when I pray
I let the candle say
more than I know.
One small puff,
one blow,
would be enough
to extinguish its light,
but it is still burning bright
when I go.

UNFAIR

It's disconcerting, to say the least,
that God is diverting into his feast
the very people who don't belong:
the weak and the headstrong,
the thief and the liar,
the murderer and the vilifier,
the selfish and the lost—
and all without cost.

There are no rights, earned or inherited,
and no guarantee,
except that God's love is unmerited
and his grace is free.

If you cite the letter of the law
you'll lose your score.
If you keep an account
your debt will mount.
If you throw good deeds into the scales
God's justice never fails.
If you are bent on achieving
you must turn round and start receiving.

Grace is unfair,
and its terror is more than pride can bear.
The heart of mission
is not prohibition,
but God's love for all without condition.

No one can bargain for what isn't priced—
this is the gospel of Christ.

DON'T SHUT THE DOOR

Are there any regrets
for missed opportunities
and wasted assets?
Any remorse for broken promises
and unpaid debts?
What about faces I have ignored,
places where I have been bored,
and music that struck no chord?
One thing gets in the way of another—
good intentions smother
good deeds, and the hours of waiting
are enervating.
Too late I respond to threats.
Sin begets sin,
I grow a thicker skin,
and even love forgets.

Lord, you require repentance and sorrow
for bewilderment today and pain tomorrow.
You demand more still:
a desire to be formed according to your will.
But don't set a deadline—
I shall only cut it too fine.
My sense of occasion is impaired,
and whenever you come I shall be unprepared
except for your grace.
So don't shut the door in my face.

UPSIDE DOWN

Lord, you say that we must lose
our lives in order to find
them, and choose
to die in order to live.
How can you justify to humankind
commands that must take captive
and control
our highest purpose and furthest goal?

You have turned
the world upside down.
You are like a fish that swims in the air,
or a lion that nests in maidenhair.
You have burned
your law into our lives like a clown
who walks
on his hands and swallows a flame
and talks
as if everyone else should do the same.

He makes us laugh
at his agility,
or else we should cry
for our fragility.
But you have acted on our behalf:
you forgive,
and when we die
you remember your glory and we live.
The dying is the hardest part—
Lord, put your law within my heart.

CONTROVERSY

If we go for a slogan
instead of a creed
the power of delusion
will cause a stampede,
feverish and hectic,
away from dialectic
to a foregone conclusion.

If we pander
to propaganda
the force of polemic
will start an epidemic—
a sickly trend
towards a dead-end.

Peremptory speech
is the easy outreach
of a blood-sucking leech.
However appealing
it promotes no healing,
but denotes a queasy lurch
towards a quasi-infallible church.

God's controversy
with us in our downfall
is about judgment and mercy
for all.
If we rely
on a partisan war-cry
the victory will be gory.

And not to us the glory.

A BLUEBIRD

In winter a shrub seems ashen,
dead. It cannot be coerced.
Before it can burst
into flower with passion,
it must wait. Before the first
gentle winds of spring
blow and the birds sing,
its twigs must be pruned back
to the ground in a beneficial attack.
It must receive—to sustain
growth—nourishment, warmth and rain.
Then at the right time,
moved by an irresistible inner cue,
the shrub comes into its prime,
clothed in a glorious array
of clear sky-blue.
The flowers sing to heaven and say:
'Glory to God who has kept his word
and given these dull branches the plumage of a bluebird.'

WAITING

Lord, we have grown weary of waiting
for the fulfilment of your kingdom
that seems lost in time's slipstream.
Behind us, like a forgotten dream,
your promises vanish in endless delay,
and ahead, like a feeble desire,
our hope has faded away.

The poor weep, the sick cry out
for healing, the hungry die every day.
The prisoners strain to hear the key
that will bring relief and set them free.
The people who live in darkness
long for the light of a new way.

Our love grows cold, and we are tired
of endurance. Peace still escapes
us and justice is long overdue.
What can you say when time rapes
our expectations? What will you do
when we seek to avenge ourselves on you?

On the cross you have spoken and acted;
there the avenger's iron rod struck a deadly blow.
The waiting seems to us protracted,
but to wait with you is to wait in the shadow
of your cross, accepting the pain,
and trusting that nothing can nullify your coming reign.

WHAT SHOULD I DO?

Lord, there is no question that holds more danger,
none more full of risk to the self-made stranger
within me, than 'What should I do?' Seizing
the time is like plunging into freezing
water so that the shock stops my breath,
or like stepping off the edge
of a precipice, bouncing on to a ledge
and falling headlong into space to my death.

The question seems to have a host of easy answers
like a hall of mirrors full of supple dancers,
until I see that it can outface me, implying
the compassionate action of your grace
that brings to the heart a merciful humbling
after days of struggling and stumbling
and nights of procrastination and sighing.
Then I fear that working it out will displace
my comfort; I have more than two coats
and plenty of the wealth that promotes
ease.

It is your generosity I contravene,
for I am looking in the wrong place at the wrong scene.
I pray: 'Your kingdom come, but not yet',
seeking self-protection from an imagined threat.
Let me gaze at the child in the manger, and at the star
hanging in the sky like a cross—a sign of how far
your love will go.

I cannot seize the time, but you
have seized me, you hold me, whatever I do.

THE SONG OF HOPE

Hope sings softly
like a mother who soothes
her baby with a lullaby,
and smooths his cheek
against a world which is bleak.
It croons gently
like an old man who praises
his first and last love readily
as they watch a butterfly.
It hums steadily
like people who toil
in a garden,
breaking the soil
so that it will not harden.
It carols persistently
like a child
who has learnt a new tune,
and practises all afternoon.

Hope is revealed
in reality, however perverse,
and reality is the love
in which God holds the universe.

Hope sings patiently
like someone who, on her sickbed,
longs for her deliverance
but comforts others instead.
Her pain does not relent,
but she accepts it
with prayerful intent.

DUST AND SALIVA

Mary, you were young
when God's holy life sprung
within you. You were lowly,
waiting quietly as the child grew slowly.

God promised a beloved son,
and you rejoiced, as we have done,
because God has lifted up the humble
and has come to help those who stumble.

You were an unmarried mother
when you conceived Jesus our brother,
heir to Israel's flesh and blood,
who, with dust and saliva, made a healing mud.

Jacob, Judah, Tamar, Rahab, Ruth,
David, Jehoram, Ahaz, Mannasseh—in truth,
liars, murderers, prostitutes and cheats,
traitors, aliens, adulterers and dead-beats.

Is there no one respectable and sincere
in the story of faith, no noble pioneer?
Jesus stands at the bottom of an inauspicious slope,
so he knows our weakness and gives us hope.

EVERGREEN

We faint for lack
of food and water
and our spirits are low.
The frozen plains
are as silent as night
and nothing will grow.
We are filled
with the fear of death
and the bitter winds blow.

The light of our lives
was born in the longest
night of the year,
when the sheep died in the fold.
Will our hearts and homes
shine with the red of forgiveness,
the green of faithfulness,
the glory of gold?
Like a fir tree
Jesus remains evergreen
even under winter's hold,
and his glory is to suffer
with all the world
the famine and the cold.

GOD IS WITH US

God is with us.
He knows the earth
and all its life,
not only as one who admires
what he has made,
but also by birth.
Our hopes and our desires
he knows, and our fears;
our sighs
and silent cries
in the shadows he hears.
God is with us
as the Gloria
is in the singing,
as the full tone
of the bell
is in the ringing,
as the circle
is in the evergreen wreath,
as the gold
is in the ribbon underneath,
as the blood red
of the holly berries
hangs over the manger bed,
as the lamb's peace,
crossbred,
is in the rejoicing
that will spread.

A BOMBSHELL

Peace fell
last night like a bombshell,
with a crack
like the sound of the rock
of ages splitting,
like the shock
of an iron hammer hitting
nails through the thin
skin
of the ringing earth,
and piercing it to its heart
with the news of a birth
and a new start.

For a crib there is the font,
roughcast, cold,
hollowed out like a hard bed
to hold
the child
in want
who is the fountainhead.

He has come so that all who have sinned
may be reconciled,
but the blast is like a bitter wind
that tosses a bird in the wild.

He is our peace
in the midst of wars that never cease.
He will bring peace at any price,
and he will be the sacrifice.

GOODWILL TO ALL

This time, I'll put aside the nativity scene
where everything is impeccably clean.
I admire the stately Renaissance caper
printed on recycled paper,
but any tableau that's worlds apart
will fail to touch my down-to-earth heart.

We need a child and we need a stable,
so let's rearrange them as a fable.
We'll have a slapstick comedy in the straw—
something impossible to ignore—
where the comings and goings of the farce
are accompanied by the braying of brass,
where acrobats turn somersaults,
and clowns on stilts lament our faults,
where banana skins and custard pies
make it unwise for anyone to moralize.

Look! God has leapt down from above
because he is head over heels in love.
He has fallen into a manger,
and his act has drawn every sort of stranger:
not saints who behave with propriety,
eyes raised to heaven, necks stiff with piety,
but sinners who laugh and cry, nonplussed,
and die in the dust, as alike we must.

Peace on earth, goodwill to all,
from the child who was born in an ass's stall,
and laughed till he cried to be so small,
and died so tall.

THE WRITING IN THE DUST

Not through reason
do we know God,
though our knowing is not unreasonable.

Not for a season
does he come,
though his coming is not unseasonable.

Gone for ever
is the notion
that I shall never
see his hand in motion.

Formerly,
the writing on the wall
said it all.

Now, normally,
the writing is in the dust—
and God with us is the God I trust.

TRAPPED IN A COCOON

Lord, you became weak—
something we scorn
to be. You speak
to us as a new-born
child more clearly
and more severely
than the wisest sage
of this or any other age.
Without uttering a word
you judge our clever talk,
showing us that it is absurd
to run before we can walk.
You are perfectly still
in the face of our perverse will.
We confine you,
but your grace responds,
and you will not undo
your bonds.
You are swaddled tight
like a body wrapped
in a grave cloth,
or like a moth
trapped
in a cocoon,
soon
in rising flight
to break free.
Lord, remember me.

STAR-CROSSED

The birth of Jesus was star-crossed,
not by two equilateral triangles
interlaced to make
a six-pointed star that dangles
like a crystal in a snowflake,
held by the frost,
nor by a five-pointed
shape which is difficult to draw
and becomes disjointed,
but by the simple star with four
points that shone above the stable door.

Anyone can draw a four-pointed star,
and even a child may demonstrate
it in his repertoire:
first make a vertical shaft or line,
then, filled with hate,
slash it through with a crossbar
to indicate something internecine—
and there you are.

The star that hung in the sky for peace
at this birth shone for love's increase.
It also shone as a cross to contradict
our enmity, foretelling bitter conflict,
suffering, death and joy beyond.
This star, this cross, is a sign of grace,
the mark of God's unbreakable bond
with the human race.

THAT'S ODD

How I hate all those phrases
that separate God from reality.
'The things of God'—
that's odd,
for everything is his concern,
and he will never spurn
the things we would hide.
He mends the heart's divide.
Nothing in our lives erases
the totality
of his participation
in the whole of his creation.
'The spiritual life'—
how can there be any strife
between spiritual and material?
We aren't ethereal;
we have no wings.
We live in mud and mire,
we shed blood,
we go through flood,
devastation and fire.
But like dust that clings,
unnoticed, to the face,
where God is all worlds interlace.

FOOTSTEPS IN THE MUD

The Lord
plunged of his own accord
into the water. He was submerged
under the tumultuous flood,
assaulted by currents thicker than blood
that surged
over his head
in the dark depths of dread.

He could hear
no voice of comfort, but chose
the roar of confusion and fear.
Then he rose
from the riverbed
as from the dead.

The Lord is enthroned over the flood,
and we can see his footsteps in the mud.

LETTING GO

It was the old who recognized
God's glory
in the temple, not the young.

Simeon prized
the ancient story
of God's presence among
his people, and age
could not defraud
him of the hope that can assuage
infirmity. Decay gnawed
at his limbs and his bones ached.
Wrinkles raked
his skin, criss-crossing
it as if embossing
a chart. He saw Christ's light
as a sign for the rising and falling
of many, a painful calling
to journey into the night.

The young are inspired
by the exploits they will achieve;
they live by brave dreaming.
The old are ailing;
their steps are slow,
their strength is failing.
But they have acquired
patience through necessity,
and, in the redeeming
light of eternity,
are making ready to let go and leave.

BELIEVING IS SEEING

Seeing is believing,
they say, and there is nothing unruly
about the things we can recognize
from the evidence of the eyes.
But, more truly,
believing is seeing,
because agreeing
to leave behind what is certain
and draw back the curtain
is a new way of perceiving,
and exchanging what is familiar
for a view of imponderabilia
is a kind of grieving.

We are comfortable in our obscurity;
we are afraid to grow towards the purity
of God's light.
But he will make us brave
enough to rise from the grave,
like the snowdrop that surprises
us as it pierces the dark earth
to shine so clean and bright
that it symbolizes
the hope of new birth.
A green spear hangs over its head,
and its petals are white
wings in the cold winter flowerbed.

Not to praise God is a kind of thieving.

SAYING AND UNSAYING

This small patch
of earth, this allotment,
this portion of land,
supports me so that I may snatch
a living by my own hand.

Here I labour somehow
to turn over the heavy clod,
the unyielding sod,
and here, between
the sweat of my brow
and the imprint of my heel,
I grow to love each recalcitrant
speck of soil as I kneel.

There is another plot
which I have not seen.
There my body will lie
and my flesh will rot.
The grass will grow green,
trees will grow overhead,
and all my saying will be unsaid.

Then I shall not say but sing
because God has given my life
and blessed it and taken it.
Then from the very stones
praises will spring.

To Christ's labouring hands,
like a speck of soil, I cling.

INDEX OF BIBLICAL REFERENCES

Many of the meditations contain several references to the Bible—some as many as six—because different meanings and connotations are linked and interwoven. This index gives the references for the main themes only.

SPRING

SUMMER

AUTUMN

WINTER

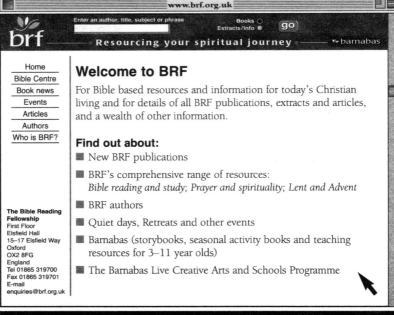

www.brf.org.uk

brf

Enter an author, title, subject or phrase

Books ○
Extracts/Info ●   **go**

Resourcing your spiritual journey ── ✿ barnabas

Home
Bible Centre
Book news
Events
Articles
Authors
Who is BRF?

Welcome to BRF

For Bible based resources and information for today's Christian living and for details of all BRF publications, extracts and articles, and a wealth of other information.

Find out about:

■ New BRF publications

■ BRF's comprehensive range of resources:
Bible reading and study; Prayer and spirituality; Lent and Advent

■ BRF authors

■ Quiet days, Retreats and other events

■ Barnabas (storybooks, seasonal activity books and teaching resources for 3–11 year olds)

■ The Barnabas Live Creative Arts and Schools Programme

The Bible Reading Fellowship
First Floor
Elsfield Hall
15–17 Elsfield Way
Oxford
OX2 8FG
England
Tel 01865 319700
Fax 01865 319701
E-mail
enquiries@brf.org.uk

Visit the BRF website at www.brf.org.uk